History of the Victoria Tunnel

This publication has been produced to celebrate the history of the Victoria Tunnel. The development of this underground waggonway as a visitor and education attraction was made possible by the programme of area-based regeneration, begun in 1997 by the Ouseburn Partnership and continued since 2007 by Newcastle City Council and since 2010 by the Ouseburn Trust..

When the Tunnel re-opened for guided tours in 2009, it was the culmination of 11 years of hard work which brought together a wide range of partners: Newcastle City Council, The Ouseburn Trust, Heritage Lottery Fund, One North East, lots of volunteers and Newcastle residents and numerous cultural attractions in the Ouseburn. Because of this financial support and community commitment, the Victoria Tunnel now has a permanent place within a vibrant Ouseburn Valley and provides Newcastle with one of its more unusual heritage attractions. In 2010 The Ouseburn Trust took over and manages the Victoria Tunnel's Guided Tours. These must be pre-booked by visiting www.ouseburntrust.org.uk or by telephone: 0191 230 4210

The Story So Far

"A Gigantic Undertaking"

When it was opened in 1835 by Messrs Porter and Latimer, the Leazes Main or Spital Tongues Colliery was one of many coal mines around Newcastle. The Industrial Revolution was in full steam: demand for coal was high and the competition was great.

Initially, the coal was carried by horse and cart from the colliery through the streets of Newcastle to the Tyne, ready for shipping. This was slow, expensive and unpopular with the Town Council and local residents. Most other collieries had their own waggonway links to the river. Porter and Latimer therefore employed a local engineer and colliery viewer, William E. Gilhespie, to plan and construct an overland waggonway, worked by horses, for Leazes Main.

In 1838, the colliery owners submitted a plan to the Town Council to construct a railroad running across the Town Moor and through Jesmond. The Council's Finance Committee felt that the construction would cause "great inconvenience and danger to the inhabitants of the town" and, more importantly, compromise the Freemen's 'herbage' or grazing rights to the Town Moor. Permission was refused.

Gilhespie's response was to propose an underground waggonway, running under the Moor, Barras Bridge, Shieldfield and down to the Tyne near the mouth of the Ouseburn. In June 1838, permission was granted and work started 12 months later.

Gilhespie retained overall responsibility for the project, while Mr John Cherry, a pitman at the colliery, was appointed to manage the excavation. Building works were carried out by the firm of Mr David Nixon, a builder based in Prudhoe Street. Up to 200 men worked tirelessly to excavate predominantly boulder clay. Using a method called 'clay-kicking' using their feet to remove the heavy clay.The Tunnel walls were lined in stone, and double brick arches provided strength beneath the floor and supported the roof.

The Grand Opening

By the 8th January, 1842, the Tunnel was finished. Thomas Fordyce in his Local Records reported that "the workmen, to the number of two hundred, were regaled with a substantial supper and strong ale, supplied by Mrs. Dixon, the worthy hostess of the Unicorn Inn, Bigg-market, Newcastle. The Albion band attended, and enlivened the joyous occasion with their music".

The Mayor of Newcastle attended the official opening on the 7th April, 1842. A crowd of spectators, including the Sheriff and important merchants, gathered on the quayside and at 1pm cannons were fired and flags waved as a train of eight wagons appeared out of the Tunnel. Four of the wagons contained coal, and the rest were occupied by "a band of musicians, many ladies and gentlemen, the engineer, and several others". The colliery owners were then congratulated on their "gigantic undertaking" and refreshments were served in a nearby marquee.

Transporting the Coal

Because of a gentle gradient in the Tunnel, loaded wagons rolled down a single standard-gauge railway track to the river. Here, there were two wooden staiths where the coal was loaded onto the waiting keels. Map of the staiths is at page 10 of this book. A long rope connected the wagons to a stationary 40hp steam engine at the Spital Tongues' site. This controlled the speed of descent and winched the empty wagons back up to the pit head.

The coal wagons were purpose-built to suit the Tunnel's dimensions. They were designed by Gilhespie and built by Hawkes & Co. of Gateshead to hold a Newcastle Chaldron (53 cwt) of coal. It was initially estimated that 12 Keels of coal per hour could be transported through the Tunnel in three runs. There are eight chaldrons to the Keel so this would require 32 wagons in each run. This proved to be over optimistic, but nevertheless, the cost of transporting the coal was dramatically reduced by nearly 90%. "What formerly cost the owners 4s. is now conveyed to the Tyne for 6d".

Accidents

The enterprise was not without its mishaps. In 1843, the haulage rope broke and the wagons "ran amain". Some wagons were lost in the river and one man was slightly injured. A recommendation followed to replace the hemp rope with a stronger wire rope, but in 1845, a similar accident involving eight wagons occurred.

At the Colliery end, the haulage engine boiler exploded twice. In 1843, the fireman, Robert Walker, was blown 50 yards away and killed. Nine years later, both the fireman, Edward Moody, and the engineman, John Burrell, were killed when the boiler blew up again.

In 1852, a potential change of colliery ownership meant that two viewers, Ralph and Benjamin Arkless required access to the Tunnel to "measure the length of it and take account of the sheaves and other stock that was in it". Accompanied by staithman William Coulson, they entered from the river. There were no passing places in the Tunnel so a message was sent to George Fletcher, the colliery underviewer, to request that no wagons were sent down during their visit.

The message failed to reach the colliery in time. Thomas Nattrass and Peter Downie were clearing the colliery site and had filled a single wagon with rubbish and small coals. The plan was to ride in the wagon and operate the brakes by hand. Downie climbed on the front, and Nattrass tried to climb on the back. Unfortunately, he tripped and fell. The wagon, however, rolled on into the Tunnel.

From his position in front of the truck, Downie was powerless; he could neither jump off nor reach the brakes.

About half way through the Tunnel, the inspection party heard the rumble of the oncoming wagon. Ralph Arkless threw himself down between the rails and survived, unhurt. His brother pressed against the Tunnel walls and suffered a broken leg. 61 year old William Coulson attempted to outrun the wagon and was killed. George Fletcher was charged with negligence.

Pit Closure

Perhaps the cost of constructing the Tunnel crippled the colliery or the coal was of poor quality and too expensive to mine, but something caused Latimer and Co. financial difficulties. As a consequence, the colliery was mortgaged to the Northumberland and District Bank on the 1st October 1848. The Bank then leased it to Thomas E. Charlton and appointed Edward Richardson as manager. In January 1857, the colliery was advertised for sale but failed to attract a buyer. The Bank was deeply affected by the world economic crisis that took place that year and by November, the liquidators had been brought in. The colliery was again advertised for sale in 1859, this time by auction. The highest bid of £6,000 failed to reach the reserve price, and the mine, its stock, plant implements and working gear was re-auctioned in 1860. It was purchased for £11,000 and operated for at least one more year by Ralph Walters.

Having taken two and a half years to build, the Tunnel was in use fewer than 20 years. In the late 1870s, the riverside end was demolished to make way for the new Glass House Bridge. Around the same time, housing in Spital Tongues was developed on the site of the former colliery and the northern end of the Tunnel was filled in.

Victoria Tunnel Mushroom Company

As far as we know, the Tunnel lay forgotten until May 1928 when Thomas Moore, an enterprising businessman from Gateshead, established the Victoria Tunnel Mushroom Company. The business closed the following year, but mushrooms were grown in the Tunnel until 1950. At this time, a Mr Hackett, of 110 Morpeth Street, Spital Tongues was renting a 300 yard section for £5 per year. When he gave his notice to terminate the lease, the Town Council thought it "advisable" not to re-let the structure.

Better Damp than Dead

In 1939, Britain prepared for war. In Newcastle, Mr Percy Parr, the City Engineer, developed plans to convert the Victoria Tunnel into a communal air raid shelter for 8,000 people. Expenditure was estimated to be £9,650. Then 16 new entrances were proposed and the estimated costs escalated to £28,100.

As always, logistics, physics and budget determined the outcome and only seven entrances were constructed. These were sited at Ouse Street, Crawhall Road,

Shieldfield Green, Ridley Place (now John Dobson Street), St Thomas' Church, the Hancock Museum and Claremont Road.

The final cost of adapting the Tunnel into an air raid shelter was at least £37,000. It was cleaned of coal dust and in some parts whitewashed. Several concrete blast walls were added to stop potential bomb debris flying along the Tunnel. Electric lighting was fitted and a new concrete floor was laid. Wooden benches and bunk beds were installed along one wall, and chemical toilets enclosed in canvas cubicles were built near the entrances.

There is no doubt that the Tunnel was a dark, damp and uncomfortable place to shelter. Many people were afraid to use it. Those that did remember sitting with their families and neighbours, exchanging gossip and often singing songs while waiting nervously for the "All Clear" from up above. In 1941, a visiting inspector reported that the attitude was "better damp than dead". He was concerned about the conditions but concluded that "as this is a mining district, the persons who will shelter in this tunnel are possibly better fitted constitutionally to resist underground and damp conditions than those in the south"!

At the end of the War, most of the fittings were removed and all of the entrances except those at Ouse Street and the Hancock Museum were closed.

Nuclear Bunker

Perhaps one reason why mushroom farming in the Tunnel stopped in 1950 was because the structure was earmarked as a potential nuclear bunker should the Cold War situation require it. No alterations were made but plans were again drawn up. These included a number of additional blast walls to protect people from a nuclear bomb.

Pandon Sewer (storm drain)

It is no longer possible to walk all the way through the Victoria Tunnel as it is bricked up at Clarence Street and at John Dobson Street. The middle section was incorporated into the city sewer (storm drain) system in the 1970s.

Restoration

A programme of visits along the 766 yards (700m) long Ouseburn section of the Tunnel was first established by the Ouseburn Partnership in 1998. The Tunnel had to close in 2006 when it began to show signs of structural strain. Funding from the TyneWear Partnership and Newcastle City Council covered the cost of repairing the damage and installing the necessary public safety measures.

Access was improved and a new programme of public tours was developed with a grant from the Heritage Lottery Fund. In April 2009, the Tunnel once again opened to the people of Newcastle.

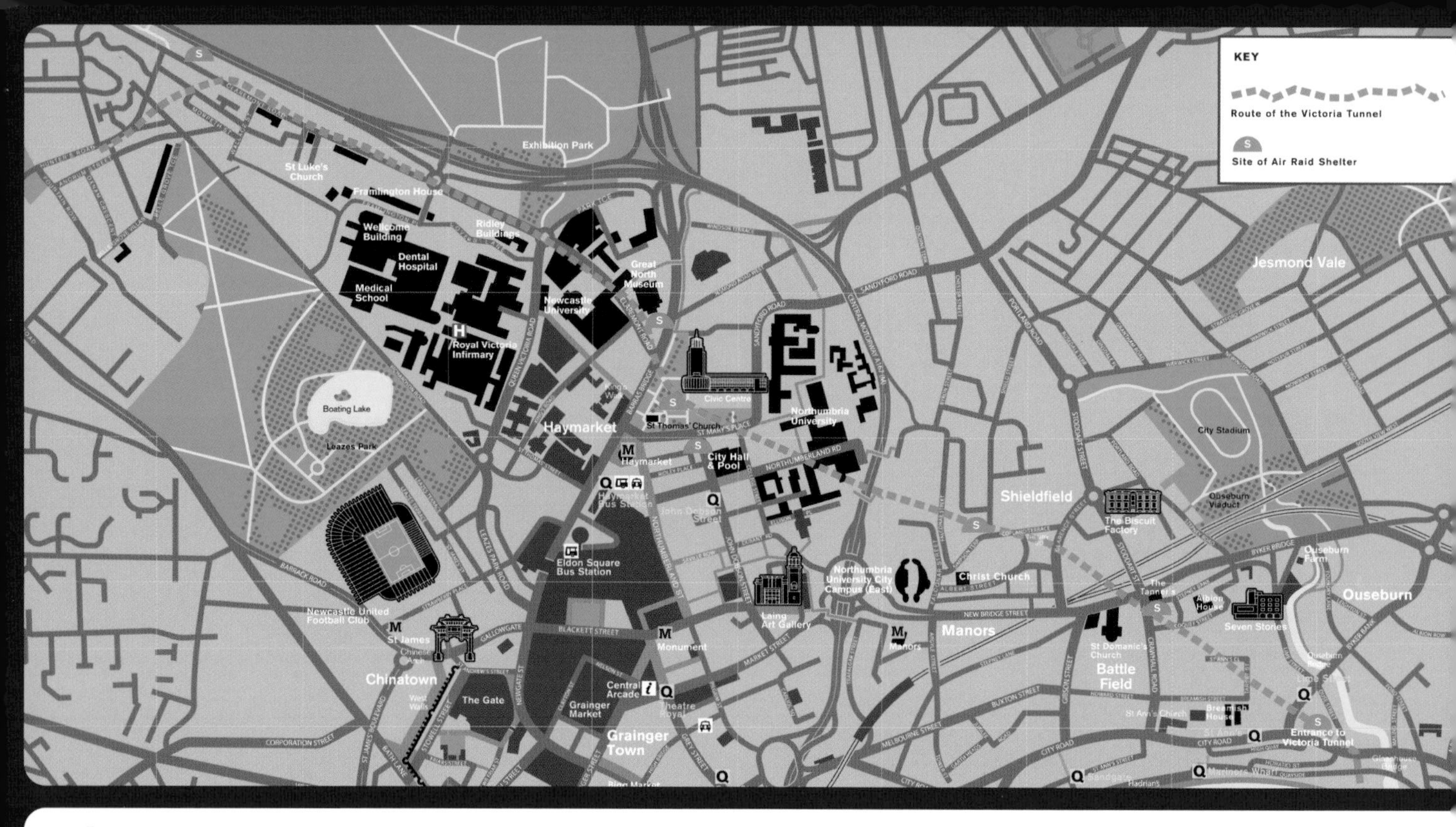

The Tunnel Route

The Tunnel runs right under Newcastle for 2¼ miles (3.6km) from Spital Tongues down to the mouth of the Ouseburn. The top and bottom entrances were filled in after the colliery closed in the late nineteenth century, but the disused waggonway can still be accessed from a WWII public entrance on Ouse Street.

City ID for Newcastle City Council. GW, NDS, Newcastle City Council 2008.

Spital Tongues Colliery

Spital Tongues or Leazes Main Colliery was sited to the north of the city centre, where Ancrum Street now stands. Fenham Barracks, Spital Tongues Ropery and Moor Lodge were nearby, but otherwise, this was an isolated location on the Town Moor. The establishment of the colliery led to the development of Spital Tongues as a small pit village.

Pencil sketch by John Wilson Carmichael. Image courtesy of Tyne and Wear Archive and Museum Service. TWCMS: B665.

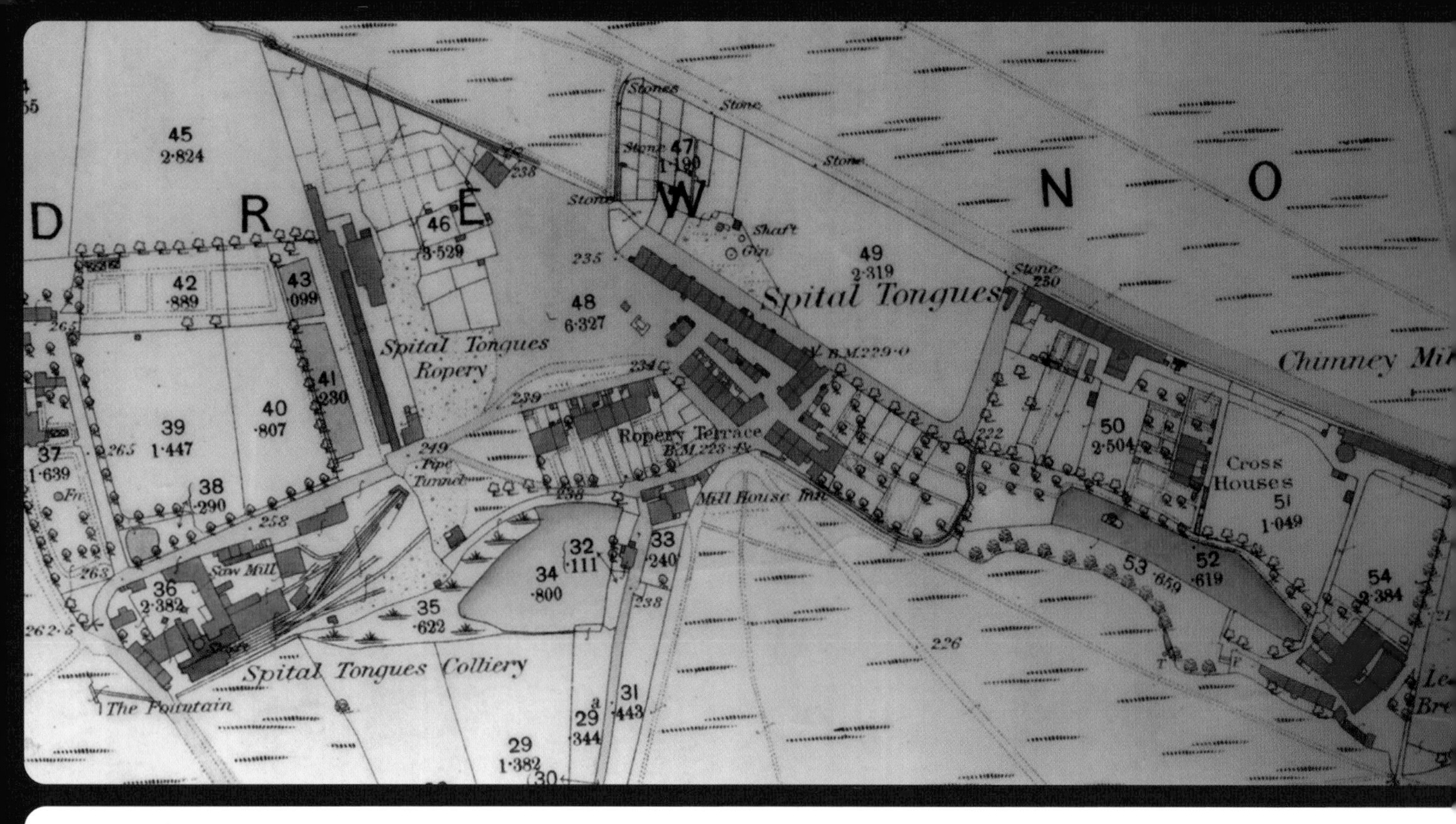

Spital Tongues, 1860

The company of Porter and Latimer was granted a 31 year lease to mine for coal under the Town Moor, Nuns Moor and Castle Leazes. The Master and Brethren of the Mary Magdelen Hospital, which owned the land around Spital Tongues, agreed to lease one acre and two roods of land for the colliery buildings.

Long Row

The colliery built two rows of terraced houses, Long Row and Short Row, for its workers. These were separated by a row of communal 'netties'. Demolished in 1906, the cottages stood roughly where Morpeth Street is now.

Their footprint is shown close to Ropery Terrace on the map opposite.

Image courtesy of Newcastle Library and Information Service.

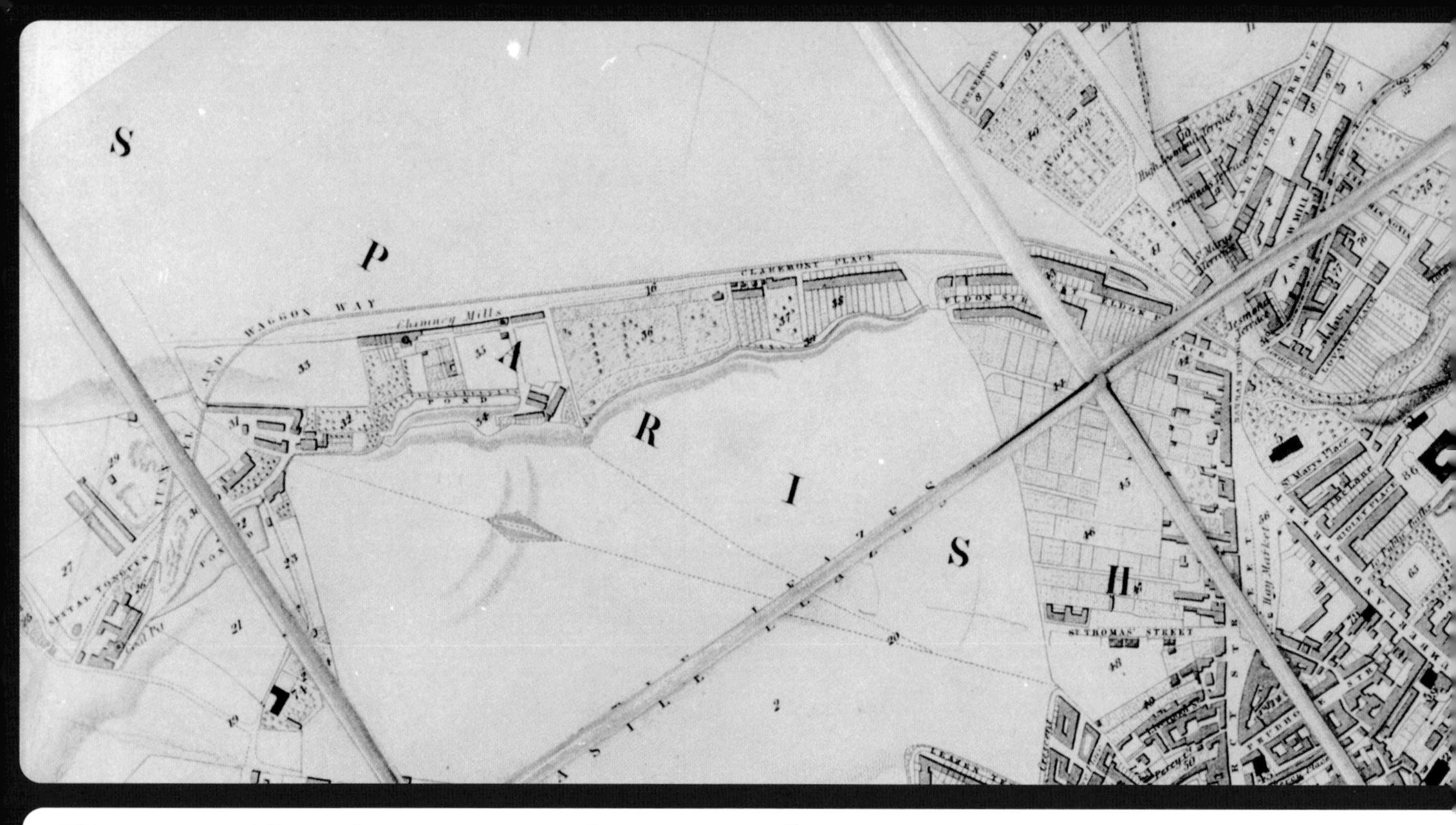

Thomas Oliver's Survey of Newcastle upon Tyne, 1844

The Tunnel took two years and ten months to construct and was completed in 1842. This was a notable achievement, hence its inclusion in Oliver's surveys of Newcastle. It is approximately 7ft. 5in. (2.3m) high and 6ft. 3in. (1.9m) wide.

At its deepest point, the Tunnel is 85 feet (26m) below the surface. The route possibly follows the course of an old stream bed as the structure was dug entirely through clay. No descriptions of the construction process survive, howev

Image courtesy of Newcastle Library and Information Service.

the method of creating tunnels at the time was to divide the work into sections. A number of vertical shafts were sunk along the proposed route and from the base of each shaft men tunnelled out to link up with the next section.

The shafts were either lined and left open for ventilation (in railway and canal tunnels) or, as is the case with the Victoria Tunnel, bricked up and backfilled. There is evidence of at least one of these shafts inside the Tunnel.

Ordnance Survey of the Ouseburn Area, 1860

At the Tyne end of the Tunnel, there was initially one wooden staith leading to the river. Here the coal was transferred from the chaldron wagons on to boats and then transported by sea to London and the wider world.

Permission to erect a westwards extension of the quay and a second set of loading gears was granted in September 1843.

Number of Certificate } ~~12308~~ 1

[Form No. 45.

"THE COMPANIES ACTS, 1908 to 1917."

Return of Allotments

of

Victoria Tunnel Mushroom Company

LIMITED,

made ~~from~~ the† 11th day of May . 1928 .

to the day of . 19 .

A Companies Registration Fee Stamp of 5s. must be impressed here.

Made pursuant to Section 88, Sub-Section 1, of The Companies (Consolidation) Act, 1908.
(To be filed with the Registrar of Joint Stock Companies within one month after the Allotment is made.)

*Distinguish between Preference, Ordinary, or other descriptions of Shares.

*Number of the Ordinary Shares allotted payable in Cash 220

* " " " " " "

*Nominal Amount of the Ordinary Shares so allotted £ 220

* " " " " £

*Amount paid or due and payable on each such Ordinary Share £ 1.

* " " " " " " " £

Number of Shares allotted for a consideration other than Cash .... } nil

Nominal Amount of the Shares so allotted .... £

Amount to be treated as paid on each such Share .... £

The Consideration for which such Shares have been allotted is as follows :—

REGISTERED
92567
13 JUN 1928

† **NOTE.—In making a return of Allotments it is to be noted that—**

1. **When a return includes several Allotments made on different dates, the dates of only the first and last of such Allotments should be entered at the top of this page, and the registration of the return should be effected within one month of the first date.**
2. **When a return relates to one Allotment only, made on one particular date, that date only should be inserted and the spaces for the second date struck out and the word "made" substituted for the word "from" after the name of the Company.**

CL 5338

TELEGRAMS: "CERTIFICATE, FLEET, LONDON" TELEPHONE: HOLBORN 0434 (2 LINES).

JORDAN & SONS, LIMITED,
Company Registration Agents, Printers, and Publishers, 162
116 TO 118 CHANCERY LANE, LONDON, W.C. 2,
and 13 BROAD STREET PLACE, E.C. 2.

Presented for filing by W. Sutton Limited Aldwych House W.C.2

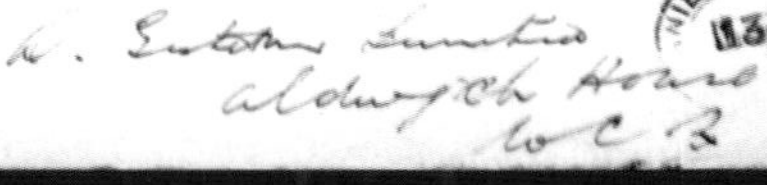

Victoria Tunnel Mushroom Company Shares Certificate

In 1928, Mr Thomas Moore established a mushroom farm in the tunnel. He leased 1,500 yards from the Town Council at a rate of £40 per annum. As both ends were now blocked, access to the Tunnel was via a wooden trap door in Ouse Street. Moore's company collapsed the following year, but other farmers grew mushrooms here until 1950.

Surveying the Tunnel, 1936

As early as January 1936, a Special Committee as to Air Raid Precautions was established and existing underground spaces such as basements, disused mines and the Victoria Tunnel were investigated as possible public shelters. The Tunnel seemed an ideal candidate: it is very close to the city centre, can hold a large number of people and is mostly more than 40 feet (12m) below the surface of the ground.

After decades of neglect, the Tunnel walls were still thick with coal dust and had in a few places partially collapsed. Nevertheless, the City Engineer's structural survey confirmed that the old waggonway was in remarkably good condition. It was sound enough to convert into a shelter.

Image courtesy of Newcastle Library and Information Service.

Constructing the Claremont Road Entrance, 1939

The first entrance at Claremont Road started as an exploratory heading because the engineers were using an old, inaccurate survey of the Tunnel. Mrs Janet Long, who lived opposite, described the celebrations when the Tunnel was eventually located. "I also seem to remember it was one of the chauffeurs coming out of the car carrying tray, glasses, also several bottles of liquid (spirits) refreshments".

Image courtesy of Newcastle Library and Information Service.

CITY AND COUNTY OF NEWCASTLE

AIR RAID PRECAUTIONS

VICTORIA TUNNEL

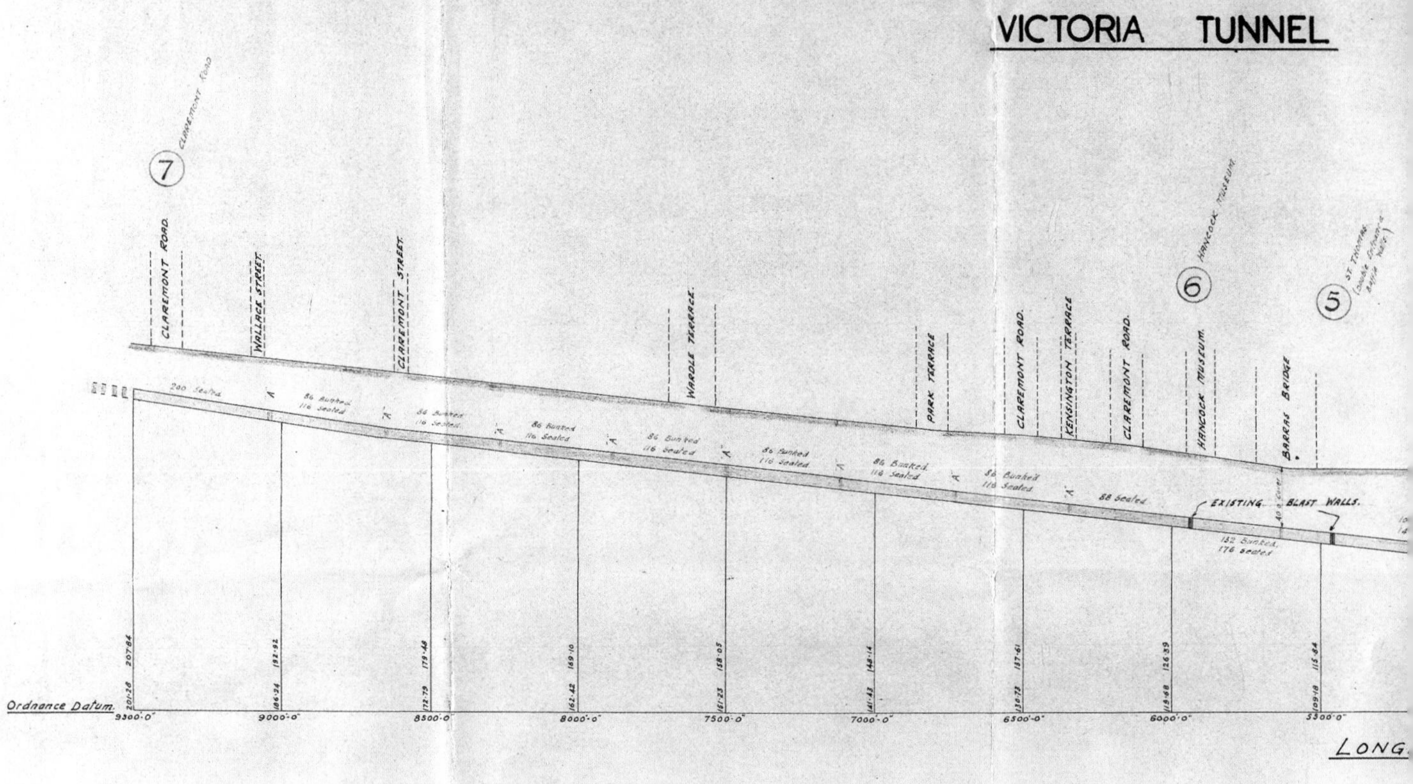

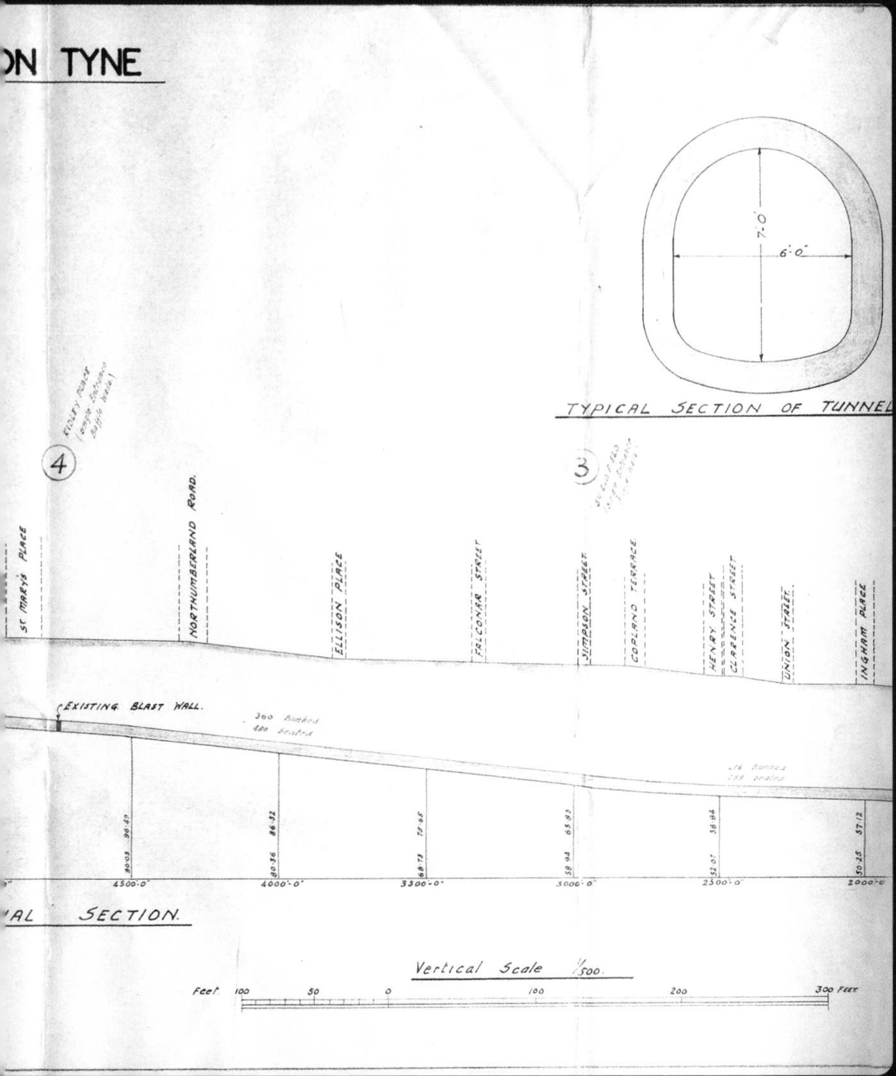

Profile of the Tunnel

On the 12th February 1939, the Sub-Committee on the Possibilities in Relation to Mining and Other Existing Deep Shelters reported that "the Tunnel after cleaning out and the shutting off of sewage gases could be utilised as a shelter, but additional entrances would have to be provided". The estimated cost of this venture was £9,650. This would provide shelter for 8,000 people at a price per head of £1.4s.0d.

This WWII profile shows the streets that the Tunnel passes under, the location of the seven completed entrances and the depth of the Tunnel underground. The number of proposed bunk beds and benches is also marked.

Image courtesy of the National Archives, Kew. WORK 28/202.

Tunnel excavation and coal transportation:

The first worker would be the 'clay kicker'; he would lie on a 45 degree angled board and remove the clay with his feet. Other workers would then remove the clay from beneath the clay kicker and move it to the surface.

Drawing and images courtesy of Jen Westcott.

When wagons had reached the staiths on the Tyne the coal was loaded onto colliers. A rapper system was used to signal the colliery and the wagons were hauled back. Evidence of that system is shown here.Together with an artists impression of a coal wagon (Chaldron).

St Thomas' Church Entrance: Building the entrance, 1940

Each entrance incorporated right-angle bends to protect the people within from nearby explosions. The gradient of these new corridors was 1 in 4, steep enough to ensure rapid access, but not so steep that it became hazardous.

During construction, new rails were laid along the Tunnel and entrance passageways so that debris and building materials could be easily transported in wagons.

Image courtesy of Newcastle Library and Information Service.

St Thomas' Church entrance: Complete 1940

"The factors deciding the height and width of the entrances were of course headroom and the number of people expected to use the shelter. 6ft. 6in. was taken as minimum headroom and the Home Office figures of 22ins. per person adopted as units of width." (Redvers W. Grant, City Engineer's Department). The entrance at St Thomas' Church was double-width because of its proximity to the city centre.

Image courtesy of Newcastle Library and Information Service.

Crawhall Road Entrance Ramp

During construction of the Crawhall Road entrance a water pipe was damaged, but the leak was mistaken for ground water saturation. Mr Bob Martin recalled how they drew "gallons and gallons of water out of the Tunnel, using a couple of cranes with big iron buckets".

Images courtesy of Mike Maguire (left) and Phil Thirkell (right).

Gas, water and electricity supplies, Post Office telephone lines and nearby buildings were damaged by subsidence. Municipal Mutual Insurance Ltd., settled a claim for £1,838.10s.10 0d." against the Corporation.

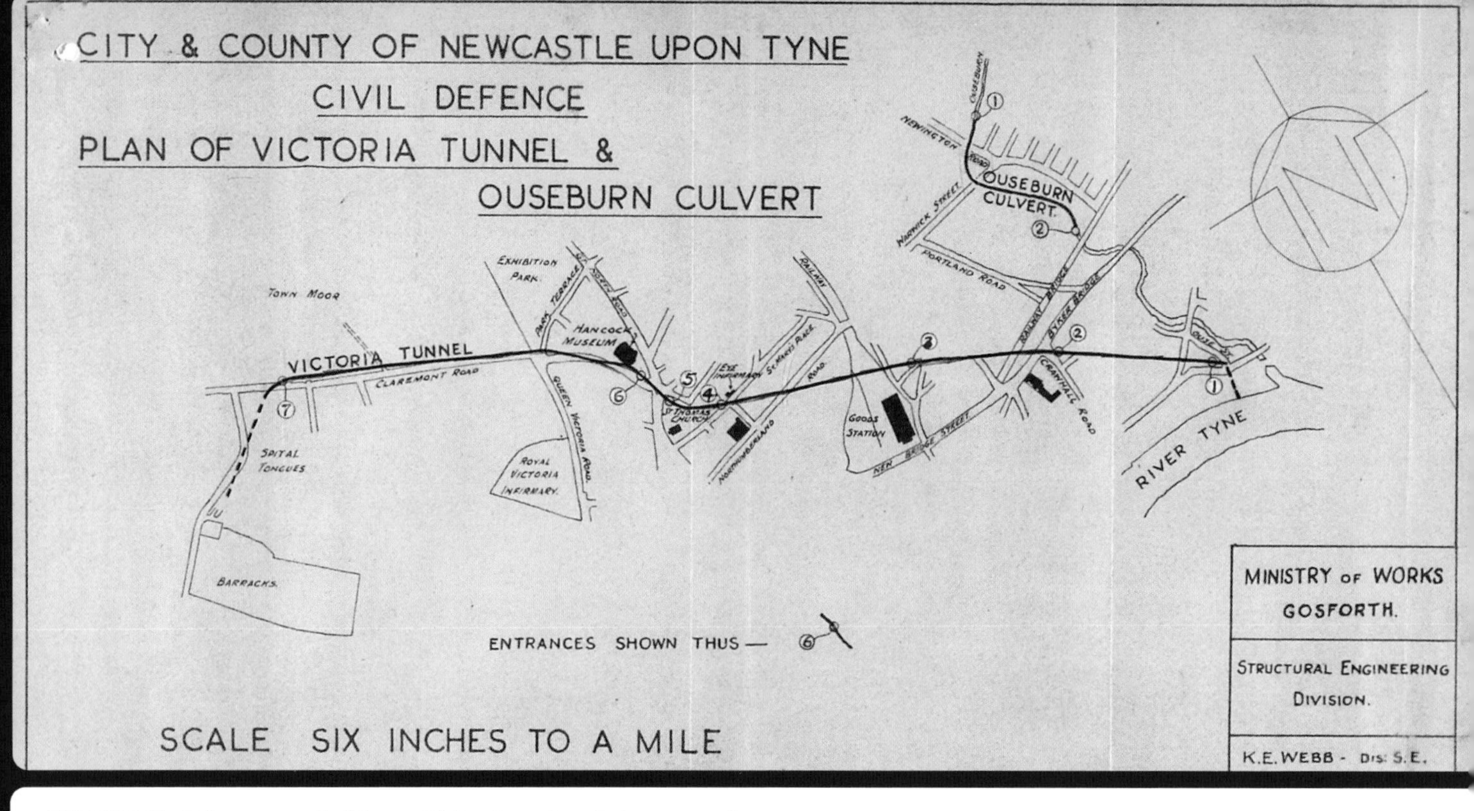

WWII Plan of the Victoria Tunnel

16 new entrances were originally proposed, but as the cost of adapting the Tunnel into a shelter reached £37,000, only seven were completed. These are marked on the above plan. The plan also outlines the Ouseburn Culvert, another underground structure adapted into a shelter. It was far more spacious than the Tunnel and included a canteen, infirmary and stage for variety shows and church services.

Image Courtesy of the National Archives, Kew. WORK 28/202.

Blast Protection and Lighting

Sections of the Tunnel walls were whitewashed and a new floor of tarmac and cement with a drainage channel down the side was laid. Blast walls were built at either end of the Tunnel where it was not deep underground.

Electric lighting ran along the ceiling and there were eight metal cupboards, each containing 20 emergency hurricane lamps sited every 400 yards (366m) along the Tunnel.

Images courtesy of Phil Thirkell (left) and Available Light (right).

Bunk Beds and Benches

Long wooden benches ran along one wall and bunk beds were also provided. Many people did not wait for a raid to start. Every night they would troop into the Tunnel with their blankets and provisions. Mrs Janet Long described how "one family had a bogie which was piled with bedding and every conceivable article . . . an alarm clock, and believe it or not the now outdated chamber pot".

Image courtesy of Newcastle Library and Information Service.

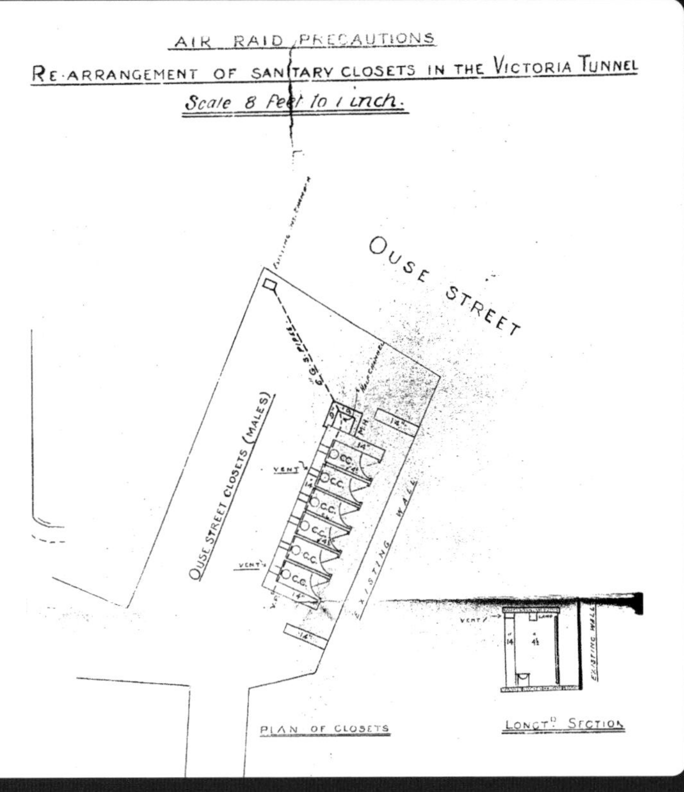

Sanitation

Chemical Elsan toilets, enclosed in canvas cubicles, were sited close to each of the new entrances – 'Ladies' on one side and 'Gents' on the other. Mr Basil McLeod remembers the strong smell of disinfectant that greeted you as you reached the bottom of the entrance ramp: "it was a bit like T.C.P., not pleasant at all".

Images courtesy of Tyne and Wear Archive and Museum Service (left) and Jen Westcott (right).

William Weddle, ARP Warden

The Tunnel was marked out in sections and ARP wardens including William Weddle (pictured), G. Brown, T. Harrison and L. Lewins patrolled during the raids and carried out servicing and maintenance duties during the day. There was also a medical aid post, and three nurses with haversacks of medical supplies toured the Tunnel to care for people who were sick or who had been injured on their way to the shelter.

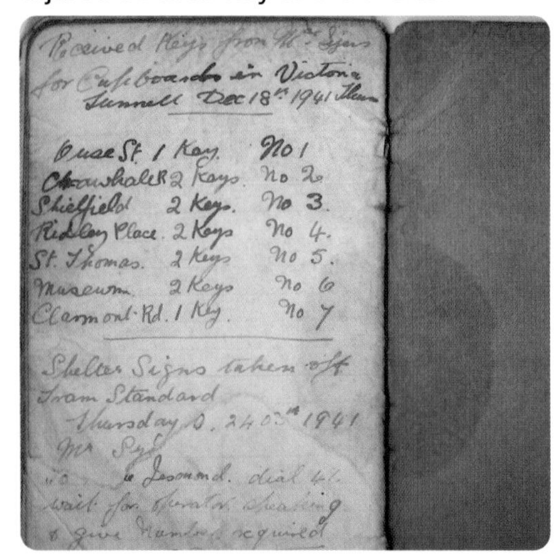

Received Keys from Mr Signs
for Cupboards in Victoria
Tunnell Dec 18th 1941 Thurs

Ouse St. 1 Key. No 1
Chowdene 2 Keys. No 2
Sheilfield 2 Keys. No 3.
Ridley Place. 2 Keys No 4.
St. Thomas. 2 Keys No 5.
Museum 2 Keys No 6
Clermont Rd. 1 Key. No 7

Shelter Signs taken off
from Standard
Thursday D. 24th 1941
Mr Sigs
[illegible] dial 4[illegible]
wait for [illegible]
& give [illegible] required

Page from William Weddle's notebook and image courtesy of Mary Archbold.

Roll of Honour

A 'Roll of Honour' and Crucifix, roughly formed in mortar, were discovered affixed to the Tunnel wall below the vicinity of St. Dominic's Church. The 'Roll' lists three names: J. Archbold, S. Stewart and B. Turner.

The surrounding masonry has been re-pointed and the initials J.A. and B.T. appear in a few places together with the date 1940. Are these the handiwork of masons involved in construction of the air raid shelter?

Images courtesy of Phil Thirkell (left) and Jen Westcott (right).

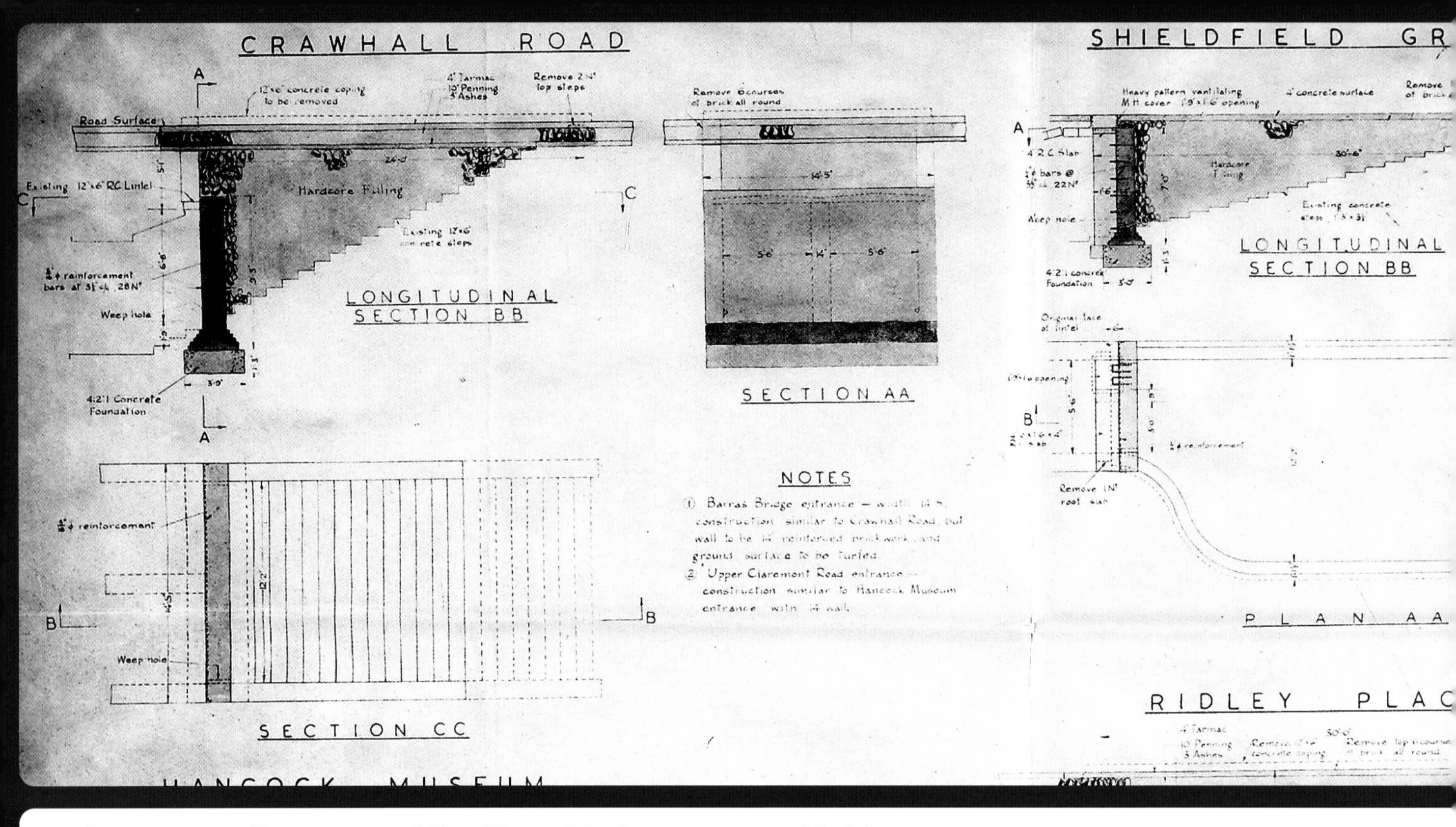

Closing of WWII Shelter Entrances, 1949

After the War, the Tunnel was stripped of its fittings and most of the entrances were filled in. Their positions were noted in case there was a need to re-open the shelter. The entrance on Ouse Street was left open because the land belonged to the Tyne Tees Shipping Company. The entrance near the Hancock Museum was also left intact and the doors can still be seen in the museum grounds facing onto Claremont Road, beside the pedestrian crossing.

Image courtesy of the National Archives, Kew. WORK 28/202.

City Engineers Inspecting the Tunnel, 1975

In 1975, the Tunnel was strengthened with concrete segments at Haymarket because the top of the new metro tunnel was less than two feet below the floor of the old waggonway. It was also in the late 1970s that Northumbria Water Authority's North Bank Interceptor Sewer bisected the Tunnel under Shieldfield.

Image courtesy of Newcastle Library and Information Service.

The Pandon Sewer Diversion, 1976

Several sewers under Newcastle required reconstruction in the 1970s. By utilising a section of the Victoria Tunnel between Queen Victoria Road and Ellison Place for the Pandon Sewer diversion, the City Engineer's Department estimated that it saved the public from a great deal of inconvenience and also around £100,000 in excavation costs. The Tunnel was lined with a concrete culvert and a number of overflow pipes were directed into it.

Image courtesy of Newcastle Library and Information Service.

Repair Work in the Tunnel, 2007

In 2006, the Tunnel began to show signs of structural strain as development works took place above it.

The damaged section was reinforced using a technique usually applied to collapsing Victorian sewers. The Tunnel walls were lined with a wire mesh and then sprayed with two layers of ferrocement. At the same time, an emergency exit was installed through the blocked WWII entrance at Crawhall Road.

Images courtesy of Phil Thirkell (top left) and Newcastle City Council.

Ouse Street Entrance, 2015

Heritage Lottery funding enabled Newcastle City Council to improve access at the entrance on Ouse Street and install a new visitor shelter containing eye-catching information boards and a tactile panel for visually impaired visitors.

Inside the Tunnel, the sounds of a wartime air raid and rumbling wagons are recreated and the presentation includes recorded recollections of local people who sheltered here.

Image courtesy of Jen Westcott.

Victoria Tunnel from Spital Tongues to under Hancock Museum.

Clockwise from top left: Entrance ramps leading to St Thomas'; the sewer pipe; Hitler graffiti; ramp under the Hancock; WW2 naughts and crosses and back-filled Spital Tongues end of the tunnel.

Images courtesy of Jen Westcott / Kerry Lister-Pattinson.

Victoria Tunnel Volunteer Guides

All guides are fully trained in Health and Safety procedures and two guides are present on all our tours.

They are very enthusiastic about the Victoria Tunnel and its history and heritage. Their dedication means that all our visitors get to see how the Victorian engineers built the tunnel and how Newcastle citizens experienced the damp and cold conditions, sheltering from bombing raids during WW2.

Without their dedication, enthusiasm and hard work these tours would not be possible. It's because of their efforts that we are so successful. If you feel you would like to join them please contact the Ouseburn Trust.

Image courtesy of Jen Westcott

Victoria Tunnel Volunteer Guides

In 2014 8900 people visited the Victoria Tunnel. Of those 1901 were under twelve year old, with 60 classes of Primary School pupils attending our WW2 and Victorian themed workshops.

Universities, colleges, scouts, cubs and lots of groups also enjoyed their Private Tours at times and dates to suit them.

Images courtesy of Eyeofthetynephotography.

A song written in 1842: THE SPITAL TONGUES TUNNEL

As aa sat i' the hoose, havin' nothing to do,
Aa heer'd the bells ringin'. Thinks aa – "What's up noo?"
Aa went to inquire, an' heer'd the folks say:
"The Spital Tongues Tunnel's been open'd today."

Chorus:
Success to the tunnel! The Spital Tongues Tunnel!
The best undertakin' that's been i' the North!

This tunnel's two miles, an' it's strange for to tell
That twenty full waggons will travel on't well;
With men for to brake them, they run doon se clivvor,
An' in less than six minutes they're doon to the river.

When first Mr. Porter began wi' this plan,
Some called him a thick-headed, mad, foolish man;
But now since it's finished each wiseacre says,
"Indeed Mr. Porter is worthy of praise."

To Latimer also great honour is due,
In backin' the project until it was through;
An' now since it's dyeun wi' the Spital Tongues Pit,
Aa hope they will syeun make a fortune by it.

'Twas Mr. Gilhespie, that famed engineer,
With Cherry an' Nixon, the tunnel did rear;
Their nyems should be thowt on as men of renoon,
An' placed on the records of wor "Canny Toon."

There here's to the owners, an' lang may they live
To enjoy what the tunnel is likely to give;
An' to each one's lady, may they aye be glad
To cheer up an' cuddle their Bonny Pit Lad.

This song was written in 1842 by Tyneside bard, Robert (Bobby) Nunn.
It was sung to the tune of "Cappy's the Dog".